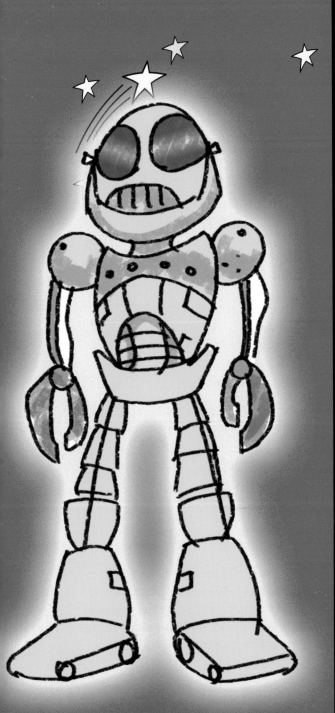

DRAW
ALIENS and
SPACE OBJECTS
in 4 Easy Steps
Then Write a Story

1
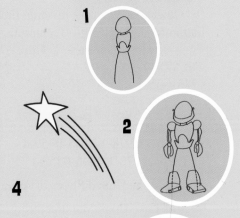

4

2

3

Enslow Elementary

an imprint of

Enslow Publishers, Inc.
40 Industrial Road
Box 398
Berkeley Heights, NJ 07922
USA

http://www.enslow.com

Stephanie LaBaff
Illustrated by Tom LaBaff

Enslow Elementary, an imprint of Enslow Publishers, Inc.

Enslow Elementary® is a registered trademark of Enslow Publishers, Inc.

Copyright © 2012 by Enslow Publishers, Inc.

Library of Congress Cataloging-in-Publication Data
LaBaff, Stephanie.
  Draw aliens and space objects in 4 easy steps : then write a story / Stephanie LaBaff
     p. cm. — (Drawing in 4 easy steps)
  Includes index.
  Summary: "Learn to draw aliens, astronauts, and space objects, and write a story about them, with a story example and story prompts"—Provided by publisher.
  ISBN 978-0-7660-3841-7
  1. Outer space in art—Juvenile literature. 2. Extraterrestrial beings in art—Juvenile literature. 3. Drawing—Technique—Juvenile literature. 4. Science fiction—Authorship—Juvenile literature. I. Title.
  NC825.O9L33 2012
  743—dc23
                           2011017565

Paperback ISBN 978-1-4644-0014-8
ePUB ISBN 978-1-4645-0459-4
PDF ISBN 978-1-4646-0459-1

Printed in the United States of America

092011 Lake Book Manufacturing, Inc., Melrose Park, IL

10 9 8 7 6 5 4 3 2 1

Illustration Credits: Tom LaBaff

To Our Readers: We have done our best to make sure all Internet Addresses in this book were active and appropriate when we went to press. However, the author and the publisher have no control over and assume no liability for the material available on those Internet sites or on other Web sites they may link to. Any comments or suggestions can be sent by e-mail to comments@enslow.com or to the address on the back cover.

♻ Enslow Publishers, Inc., is committed to printing our books on recycled paper. The paper in every book contains 10% to 30% post-consumer waste (PCW). The cover board on the outside of each book contains 100% PCW. Our goal is to do our part to help young people and the environment too!

Contents

Getting Started

Lots of Paper →

Pencil sharpener →

Your imagination →

↑ Pencil

Eraser ↓

Drawing aliens is as easy as 1, 2, 3, 4! Just follow the 4 steps for each picture in this book. You will be amazed at what you can draw. After some practice, you will be able to make your own adjustments, too. Change a pose, move a leg, or draw a different alien. There are lots of possibilities!

Follow the 4 Steps

1 Start with big shapes, such as the body.

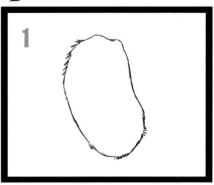

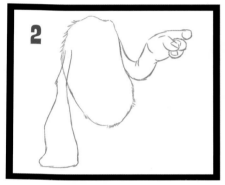

2 Add smaller shapes, such as the arms. In each step, new lines are shown in red.

3 Continue adding new lines. Erase lines as needed.

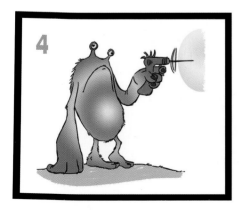

4 Add final details and color. Your alien will come to life!

Astronaut

1

2

Erase the dotted line behind his helmet and gloves.

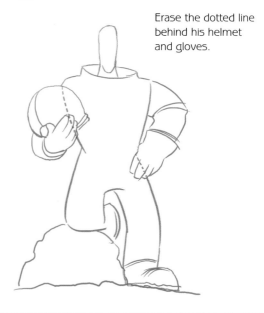

3

4

Astrogirl

1

2

3

Erase the dotted line behind her lasers, boots, and neck.

4

Astrodog

1

The legs are always tricky, so take your time.

2

Erase the dotted lines behind the legs.

3

Erase the dotted line behind the ears and spacesuit.

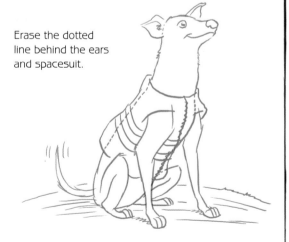

4

Spacesuit

1

2

Erase the dotted line behind the gloves.

3

Erase the dotted line behind the helmet.

4

Snarkle

1

2

3

Add sticky tentacles.

4

Scruff him up a bit if he looks too clean.

Blinky

1

2

3

Erase the dotted line behind the nose.

4

Dogger

1

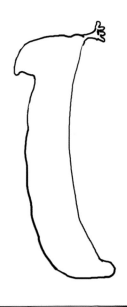

2

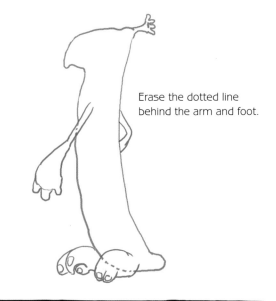

Erase the dotted line behind the arm and foot.

3

4

Goobie

1

2

3

4

Bleet

1

2

3 Erase the dotted line behind the gun, eye, and arm.

4

Catarian

1

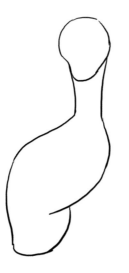

2

The bigger the eyes, the more alien she'll look.

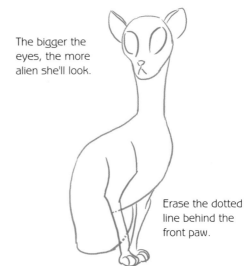

Erase the dotted line behind the front paw.

3

Erase the dotted line behind the leg and tail.

4

Try your own crazy color combination!

Visilla

1

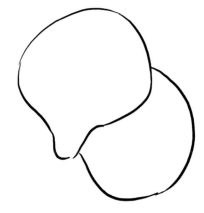

2

Make her head and feet big
so she looks young.

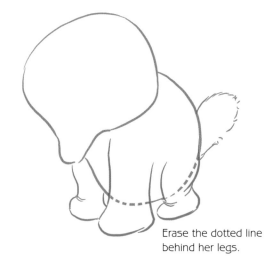

Erase the dotted line
behind her legs.

3

4

Buzzer

1

Take your time with this shape.

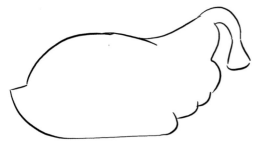

2

Then the details are easy!

3

4

Hive

1

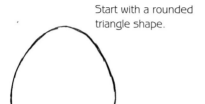

Start with a rounded triangle shape.

2

3

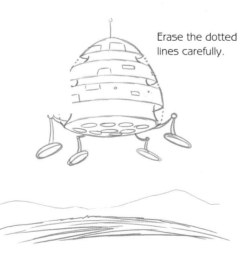

Erase the dotted lines carefully.

4

Space Capsule

1

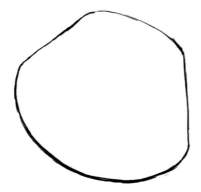

2

Erase the dotted line behind the cube shape.

3

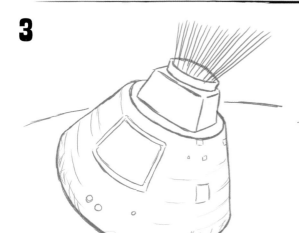

4

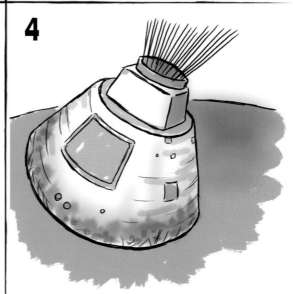

Crasher

1

2

3

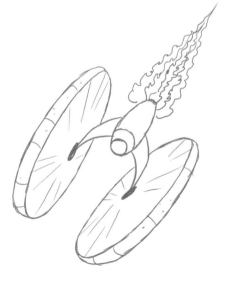

4

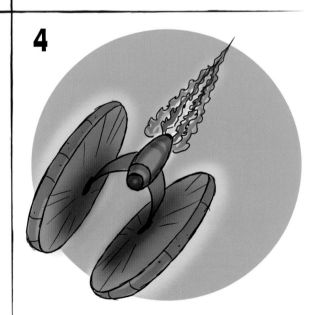

Space Shuttle

1

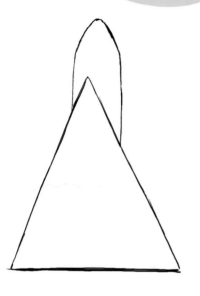

2

Erase the dotted line triangle shape.

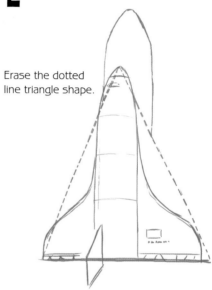

3

Erase the dotted line at the base of the rocket.

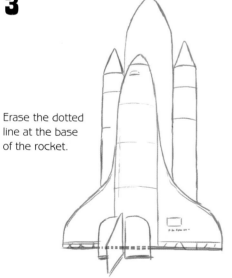

4

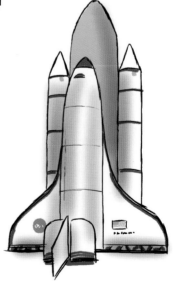

Fighter

1

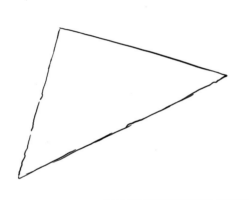

2

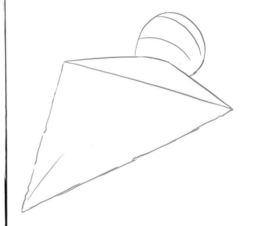

3

Erase the dotted line
behind the bullet shape.

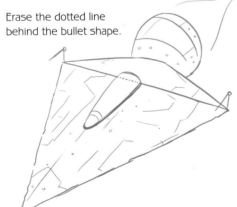

4

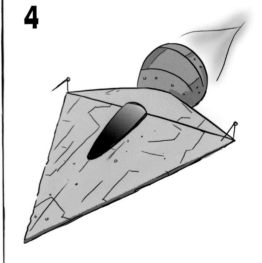

Rocket

1

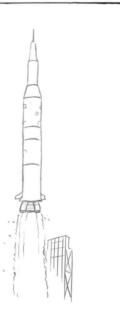

2

3

4

Satellite

1

2

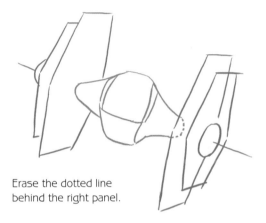

Erase the dotted line
behind the right panel.

3

Erase the long dotted
line behind the panel.

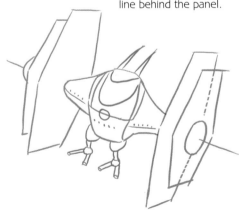

4

Ninja Fighter

1

Start with the shape of a slipper.

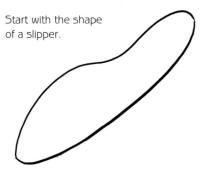

2

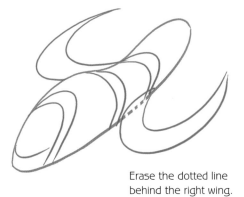

Erase the dotted line behind the right wing.

3

Use thin lines for surface texture.

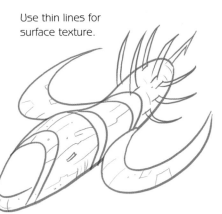

4

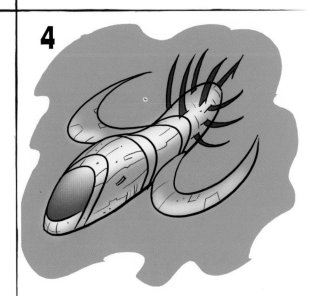

Turbo Fighter

1

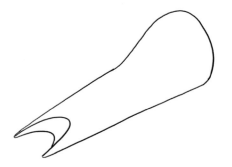

2

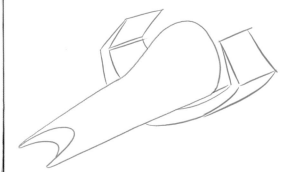

3

Adding the little surface details is easy and makes it look real!

4

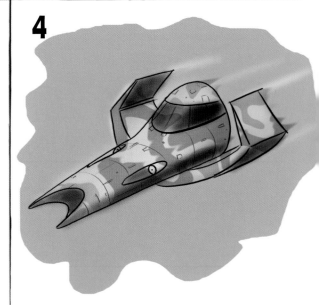

Gunbot

1

2

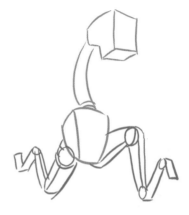

3

Erase the dotted line
behind the shoulder.

4

Robot

1

2

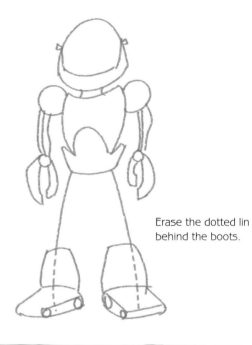

Erase the dotted line behind the boots.

3

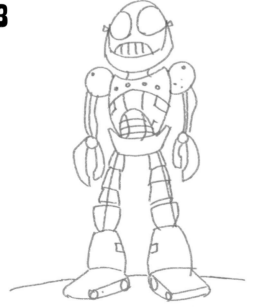

4

Botkin

1

2

3

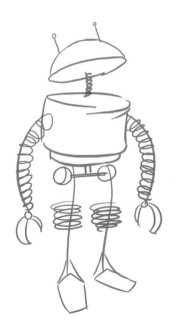

4

Rover

1

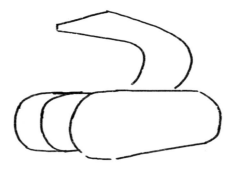

2

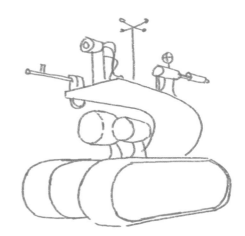

3

4

Satellite

1

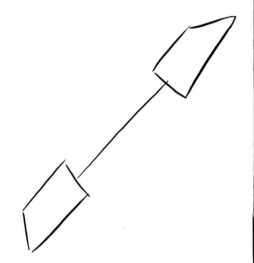

2

Erase the dotted line at the center of the satellite.

3

4

Ground Tank

1

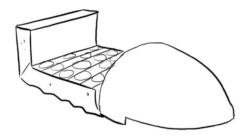

2

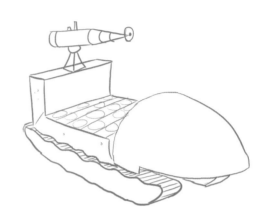

3

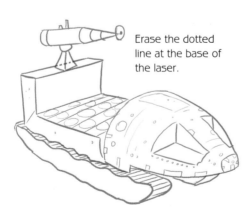

Erase the dotted line at the base of the laser.

4

Meteor

1

Start with a small imperfect ball in the corner.

2

Meteors disintegrate as they enter Earth's atmosphere.

3

Add a vapor trail.

4

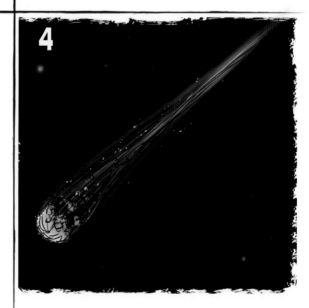

Moon

1

Ready for an
easy one?

You can use a cup
for the circle, but it's
okay to have wobbly lines.

2

3

Rough up the surface.

4

Throw in some color!

Saturn

1

2

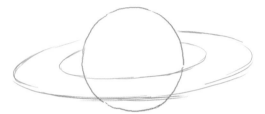

3

The rings are transparent, so there is no need to erase behind them.

4

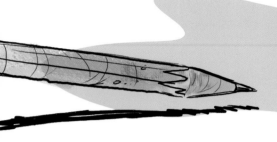

How to Write a Story

Write a Story in 5 Easy Steps

Are you ready to write a story to go with your drawings? Maybe you have a story you want to illustrate. Follow these five simple steps to make your very own story with drawings.

Step 1: Prewriting

Do you want to write about aliens? Maybe you have an idea for a story about aliens in outer space. Keep in mind the drawings you want to use and base your story around them.

One way to begin your story is to answer these questions: Who? What? Why? Where? When? How?
For example:
Who is your alien?
What happens to it in your story?
Why is its story interesting?
Where and when does it live?
How does it react to its situation?

Here is a good brainstorming exercise. Fold a paper into six columns. Write the words *Who? What? Why? Where? When?* and *How?* at the top of each column. Write down every answer that comes into your head in the matching column. Do this for about five or ten minutes. Take a look at your list and pick out the ideas that you like the best. Now you are ready to write your story.

Alien Story Starters

I watched the strange ship land in our yard. Nothing exciting usually happens here on Mars . . .

The spaceship was badly damaged in the meteor shower when . . .

We had just landed on the Moon when a strange creature walked up . . .

The fighter came shooting toward the spaceship. We were under attack . . .

As I walked down the hall in the space station. I couldn't believe I was seeing these strange . . .

Step 2: Writing

Use the ideas from the list you made in Step 1. Write your story all the way through. Don't stop to make changes. You can always make changes later.

A story about an alien flying around in space isn't very interesting. What could happen to this alien? What if there were a meteor getting ready to crash into its planet? Think of all of the things that could go wrong. Your story will be more exciting if you don't make things too easy for the alien.

Step 3: *Editing*

Read your story. Is there a way to make it better? Rewrite the parts that you can improve. You might want to ask a friend or teacher to help. Ask them for their ideas.

Step 4: *Proofreading*

Make sure the spelling, punctuation, and grammar are correct.

Storyboarding

Check to see that your story works with your drawings. Find a table or other flat surface. Spread your drawings out in the order that goes with your story. Then place the matching text below each drawing. When you have your story the way you like it, go to Step 5. You can pick a way to publish your story.

Step 5: *Publishing Your Book*

You can make your story into a book.
There are many different forms your book
can take. Here are a few ideas:

⭐ Simple book – Staple sheets of blank paper
together along their edges.

⭐ Folded book – Fold sheets of blank paper in
half, then staple on the fold.

⭐ Hardcover book – Buy a blank hardcover
book. Then write your finished story in the book,
leaving spaces to add your art.

⭐ Bound book – Punch a few holes along the
edges of some pieces of paper. Tie them up or
fill the holes with paper fasteners. There are
many fun and colorful binding options at office
supply stores.

⭐ Digital book – Create a digital book using your computer. There are some great programs available. Ask an adult to help you find one that is right for you.

Our Story

You have finished the five steps of writing and illustrating a story. We bet you created a great story! Want to see ours? Turn the page and take a peek.

Astrodog Saves the Day

Astrogirl stumbled from the smoking wreckage of her spaceship. The engines had been badly damaged during the meteor shower, and she had barely made it to the planet's surface before they lost all power.

"Where do you think we are, boy?" she asked her trusted companion, Astrodog. But when she looked down, he was not there. Astrogirl looked around—nothing. Astrodog had disappeared!

"Just great," she muttered. "First a crashed spaceship, and now a missing dog."

She began to search. "Astrodog! Where are you?" she called as she walked up a small hill. But when she got to the top, what she saw stopped her dead in her tracks.

She was face-to-face with the strangest looking cats she had ever seen. They had the body of a cat, but their huge eyes were neon green, and their stripes were bright shades of purple and blue.

Astrogirl gasped. "Catarians!" She had learned about this alien species in space school. And although they might look like exotic pets, they were some of the meanest creatures in the galaxy.

Astrogirl was in big trouble. The Catarians began to move closer to her, hissing and bearing their sharp claws.

Thinking fast, Astrogirl pulled out her laser gun and aimed it at the largest Catarian. She fired. The laser bounced right off its catlike body. "Rats," she thought. "I forgot that Catarians are immune to laser beams!" Now what? If she didn't act fast, she'd be shredded to bits!

Suddenly, there was a noise behind them. They turned to see what it was. It was Astrodog! When he spotted the Catarians about to pounce on Astrogirl, he let out a

blood-curling howl. The Catarians' hair stood on end, and they turned and ran away over the hills. "Of course," thought Astrogirl. "It's the one thing that space cats are not immune to—space dogs!"

Astrodog came bounding over to his owner and covered her face with dog kisses. Astrogirl laughed. "Boy, am I glad to see you! You saved the day! Now let's go fix that spaceship so we can get off this planet."

Further Reading

Books

Arnold, Tedd. Green Wilma, Frog in Space. New York: Penguin Group, 2009.

Cook, Janet. How to Draw Robots and Aliens. Tulsa, Okla.: EDC Publishing, 2006.

Daley, Michael J. Space Station Rat. New York: Holiday House, 2005.

Landry, Leo. Space Boy. New York: Houghton Mifflin, 2007.

McNulty, Faith. If You Decide to Go to the Moon. New York: Scholastic, 2005.

Internet Addresses

NASA. Grades K-4. 2011.
<http://www.nasa.gov/audience/forstudents/
k-4/index.html>

National Geographic. Solar System. 2010.
<http://science.nationalgeographic.com/science/space/
solar-system>

Yahoo! Kids. Galactic Glossary. 2011.
<http://kids.yahoo.com/science/space>

Index